RETURNING TO GOD

The Life of Abba Moses the Strong

FR. MAKARIOUS ABBA MOSES

THE PARTHENOS PRESS

Contents

Foreword   5

Introduction   7

CHAPTER ONE
Early Life   11

CHAPTER TOW
The Confession of Moses   18

CHAPTER THREE
His Struggle in the Virtues   25

CHAPTER FOUR
Lessons Learned from the Life of St. Moses   32

CHAPTER FIVE
The Sayings of St. Moses   36

Appendix: Hymns for Abba Moses the Strong   44

Bibliography   53

Foreword

The spiritual elder, John Saba, once said, "Blessed is repentance, for it transforms adulterers into virgins." It is truly hard to imagine our lives without repentance because that would mean eternal death. However, God in His love has given us holy repentance that we may return to Him once more and receive eternal life.

Repentance is not only a second chance, but it is the help and work of the Holy Spirit. Repentance is the work of God in the life of a sinner. The Holy Scripture says, "You have chastised me, and I was chastised, like an untrained bull; restore me, and I will return, for You are the LORD my God."[1] The Holy Spirit rebukes sin and guides the person on the path of repentance. He provides him with grace to struggle and overcome sin. He strengthens him for spiritual warfare and victory over sin, and supports him with power and blessings to continue in the life of struggle and victory.

---

1   Jeremiah 31:18.

The story of St. Moses is a wonderful example of how to lead a life of repentance. It is a strong proof of the work of the Holy Spirit in the life of the sinner and His guidance to a life of repentance. It is a story of hope for anyone fighting sin, and St. Moses is a role model to follow in the life of victory.

This book tells us the story of the great fighter St. Moses and beneficial lessons from his life, especially those of repentance and his return to God.

We thank Reverend Father Makarious Abba Moses, the monk-priest, for writing this blessed account. I ask God to reward him with the heavenly reward, and bless these words with His Holy Spirit that they may yield fruit, thirty, sixty, and a hundred fold; through the intercessions of St. Mary and the great among the saints, St. Moses the Strong, and the prayers of His Holiness Pope Tawadros II. All glory and honor be to our God forever. Amen.

Youssef
Servant of the Monastery of St. Mary and St. Moses, Corpus Christi, TX

Introduction

Remembering the lives of the saints is a strong motivation for everyone to unite with God. For out of His love, God has given us these examples so that we may learn from the heroes of these stories how to change our lives for the better. "Remember those who rule over you, who have spoken the word of God to you, whose faith follow, considering the outcome of their conduct."[2]

This book is not written just to praise St. Moses or to tell his story, but its main goal is to send a message to all those who are far from God and feel that they have no hope of returning to Him. God has given us many stories of people who lived far from Him, and whose lives have changed, like the great St. Moses, St. Paesia, St. Augustine, St. Mary of Egypt, and many others who have become living examples for us, inspiring us to change. We notice that upon hearing the heavenly call, all these saints

---

2   Hebrews 13:7.

repented without hesitation and speedily returned to the knowledge of the way: "I will arise and go to my father, and will say to him, 'Father, I have sinned against heaven and before you.'"[3]

The life of St. Moses is an example of a life of a sinner who repented, returned to his senses, and walked in the path of virtue, which consists of the following four steps:

The first step is humility and regret, where a person blames and judges himself.

The second step is hope; one must never lose heart because the door to repentance is always open.

The third step is confession of sins and judgment of oneself with bitterness, without looking for excuses. One must also confess to God at the hand of a priest, to whom God gave the authority to loose and bind sins. Therefore, confession must not turn into chatting, regardless of how close a person may be with the priest. In the Mystery of Confession, one ought to bow before God, in tears and humility, and with true intentions. One must make a vow with God to never return to the path of sin and must renew their covenant with Him. Confession should be taken seriously, and one must confess to God at the hand of the priest, as Joshua the son of Nun said to Achan the son of Carmi.[4] Confess to God at the hand of the priest, for the law is requested out of the

---

3   Luke 15:18.
4   See Joshua 7:19.

mouth of priests, for they are prophets of the Lord of hosts, not because of their piety but because they are priests of the Most High.

The fourth step is to have true intentions for the renewal of life through repentance. Repentance means to return, and doing so means to change one's way and reverse direction. If your life continues sinfully, how can it be called repentance? Get rid of your old life, including all the bad habits and all the friends who tie you to sin. That is why the Coptic and Greek word "metanoia" means a change of mind. Therefore, unless there is a change of one's mind or intention, there is no repentance.

As a measure of how true our repentance is, a person can ask oneself in truth, "If there was a chance to sin, would I fall again?" Or, "Would I remain unsure?" Or, "Would I not fall by the grace of God?"

The first answer means that there is no repentance at all. The second answer means that the repentance is incomplete. But the third answer means that the repentance is complete and true.

St. Moses was faithful, serious, and strong in his repentance. He is called "the Strong," not because of his physical strength but because of the strength of his repentance. He changed from being an evil person to a person who has God's Spirit in him, from a thief and a robber to a gracious giver and a host to strangers. He used to carry a sword, but now carried a cross. Repentance is the act of purifying oneself from all sin, without returning to it again.

We thank God, who has given us hope and repentance in every case and every circumstance. Repentance is one of God's greatest gifts to people. If one sins in any way, then it is the means for the renewal of soul, spirit, and body. It returns the person to purity as the Spiritual Elder said: "Repentance transforms an adulterer into a virgin." It fills the person with peace and joy. Also, the heavens rejoice at the repentance of any sinner: "I say to you that likewise there will be more joy in heaven over one sinner who repents than over ninety-nine just persons who need no repentance."[5]

May God grant us to follow the example of His saints and change our minds and hearts, and guide us to the life of repentance through the intercessions of our loving mother and the pride of our race, St. Mary, St. Moses the Strong, and all the hosts of the heavenly orders, saints and martyrs; and the prayers of H.H. Pope Tawadros II and his partner in the apostolic service H.E. Metropolitan Youssef, Metropolitan of the Coptic Orthodox Diocese of the Southern United States and Abbot of the Monastery of St. Mary and St. Moses in Texas. May the Lord bless their lives for many years in peace and tranquility. Amen.

Makarious Abba Moses

---

5   Luke 15:7.

1

Early Life

The name Moses (Coptic **Ⲙⲱⲥⲏ**) is Pharaonic, a Coptic name. It is divided into two parts: The first part "**Ⲙⲱ**" (Mo) means "water," and the second part "**ⲥⲏ**" (see) means "son." Therefore, the name **Ⲙⲱⲥⲏ**, means "son of water" or "the one taken out of the water."

It is not known where Moses was born; some say he was a barbarian, and very little is known of his childhood. His youth had nothing promising. He lived from approximately AD 330 to 407. He was a pagan who especially worshipped the sun. He had black skin and was a servant of a high authority figure until his master became angry with him for his evil ways and thievery and cast him out. This is the story of his life after his master cast Moses out of his house.

After being cast out, Moses led a gang of thieves

and became a murderer who depended on his bodily strength. He was very tall, to the point that upon his death, they could not find a coffin large enough, so they had to bend his legs to be able to fit him into one. He was very broad in stature and was as strong as a wrestler. He lived according to the laws of the jungle: bullying, thievery, robbery, and murder. No one could confront him because he was exceedingly frightening. He dwelt in the mountain with his followers, who gathered around him and became his gang.

The following is a story that shows the extent of his evil ways: A shepherd and his dogs once kept Moses from getting to the shepherd's sheep, and so Moses despised the shepherd. Moses then decided that he would kill the man, so he searched for his flock. He found the flock across the Nile River, which was at the peak of its flooding at that time. He swam one mile across the river with his sword between his teeth. The shepherd, seeing him from afar, hid in the sand. Moses chose four large sheep, slaughtered them and tied them all with one rope and swam back with them across the river! He skinned them and ate most of their meat, then sold their skin to buy alcohol, which he drank in large quantity. He then walked fifty miles to return to his gang and awoke very late the next morning due to the large quantity of alcohol that he had drunk. It is also said that he killed a hundred people, and he was gluttonous, prone to excessive eating and drinking alcohol. He led a life full of robbery, robbing the convoys that passed by on the major roads.

The Call of Heaven

It happens to people, even criminals and murderers, at certain moments, that God touches their hearts. This is because humans are originally created in God's image. If people are capable of taking advantage of these moments and hold on to the tip of this rope, they will be able to get out of the swamp of sin.

One moonless night, with a clear sky and bright stars, Moses was meditating on the sky and the stars, which were geometrically arranged. He asked himself, "What is this dome? What is all this beauty? Who made this universe, and who controls it? Why do these stars not plummet to the ground?" These questions and many more perplexed him. We realize now that God opened Moses' eyes, and he started to feel that the universe must have a Controller. He longed to know Him. The next morning, Moses looked at the sun, which was the only god he knew. He spoke to it, saying, "O sun! If you are the true god, inform me." However, he pondered, saying, "How can you be god, if when the night comes, you vanish? There must be a mighty God who has created all these things." Another time, he asked God, "O God, whom I do not know, make me aware of your existence."

This issue vexed him, and he wanted to find an answer to it, so he descended the mountain to ask someone, but whenever he came near anybody, they feared that he might kill them, and they ran away. He became very upset because he felt hated, and he could not live with this feeling any longer. It is here that God's hand started to work in him.

After a while of confusion, some people told him, "If you desire to find the answers to these questions, go to the monks who are dwelling in the wilderness of Scetis (Shiheet)." At this advice, he quickly went to the wilderness of Scetis to look for these monks to learn from them who the true God is, and he continued to search the desert until he found a monastery.

Moses knocked on the gate, and the gatekeeper asked him how he could help him. Moses replied, "I want to meet the head of the monastery."

The gatekeeper replied, "The abbot is in the church." Moses asked if he would be permitted to enter the church and was told, "First, you must leave your sword outside."

Moses replied, "I do not need it." Then the gatekeeper allowed him in. The monks had heard of Moses, but had never before seen him, and they found him to be very tall, strong, and black.

Upon entering the church, Moses found the abbot giving a sermon, and according to God's will, the sermon was about judgment and the fate of the person after death. Moses was amazed by the words he heard, and because it was the first time he had heard such things, he was terrified of the judgment. He realized that no matter how mighty he was, there must be someone mightier. There will be a day for judgment on which his pride will be broken, and his days will come to an end.

He could not control himself and was incapable of waiting any longer, so he loudly asked, "What if someone wishes to repent?"

St. Isidore replied, "He must confess his sins, so that he may start a new life," and then continued his speech.

However, Moses interrupted him again, saying, "I wish to repent now." St. Isidore told him to wait until the end of the sermon, but Moses quickly replied, "What if I die now?"

At this, St. Isidore was embarrassed, so he ended the sermon and dismissed the monks. He approached Moses and asked him, "What is your story?"

Moses said, "I am Moses the Strong, the leader of a gang of thieves. I am a murderer. I have killed many and stolen much and have done every evil thing."

St. Isidore asked him, "What can I do to help you?"

Moses said, "I wish to learn everything about God." St. Isidore asked what he used to worship previously, and Moses replied, "I do not know God, but I used to worship the sun, because I noticed that it illuminates the world. However, the night comes, and it is no longer there. Likewise, the moon and the stars contain many mysteries, along with the sea and all its strength. All these things proved to me that there is a strong God who is the creator and controller of the world." St. Isidore asked if that was the reason he was there, and Moses confirmed that it was so.

St. Isidore told him about God and the extent of His love for mankind, and that He gave His only-begotten Son for the salvation of the world. He also told him about the mercies of God and the Day of Judgment, and how God will reward each one according to his deeds. God touched Moses' heart, and he asked St. Isidore, "My life is filled with evil; if I die now, how can I face God?"

St. Isidore told him, "There is a path for repentance, and the path is available. The door to heaven is always open, as the Lord says, 'I did not come to call the righteous, but sinners, to repentance.'"[6]

Moses asked, "Is it possible for me as well?"

St. Isidore replied, "Yes. The Lord forgave all the sins of the right-hand thief as well when he repented on the cross. God is a tender-hearted, merciful, and loving Father. He is willing to accept the person if

6   Mark 2:17.

he truly repents. 'The one who comes to Me I will by no means cast out.'"[7]

Moses decided to leave his evil companions whom he used to lead, and he continuously occupied himself with fervent regret for his evil ways. St. Isidore took him to St. Macarius the Great, who took him under his care and blessed him, then sent him back to St. Isidore to be baptized and to continue to learn from his teachings. This is because St. Isidore was the priest of Scetis and was responsible for the new monks. He was also a disciple of Abba Macarius and was especially patient with sinners; therefore, he was the spiritual guide of Scetis.

---

7   John 6:37.

2

The Confession of Moses

All the monks gathered in the church, and Moses knelt and confessed his sins out loud before all, weeping with tears of regret. While he was confessing, St. Macarius saw an angel on the altar of the church holding a slate as black as coal. As Moses confessed at the hands of St. Isidore, the angel would erase with his finger a line on the slate, and it would turn white. The more Moses confessed, the whiter the slate became, until it became completely white. When Abba Macarius saw this vision, he relayed it to St. Isidore to confirm to him the genuineness of Moses' repentance. Afterwards, about making Moses confess publicly, some monks asked St. Isidore, "Why did you allow such a scene to take place before the monks?"

St. Isidore replied, "I did this for two reasons. First, to save Moses from the embarrassment and to allow him to face the other monks. Second, because some monks have sins that they have not yet confessed, and through this, they may be encouraged to confess, because without confession, there would be no forgiveness or entry into heaven."

The Change of Life after Repentance

After Moses the Strong's true repentance and Baptism, St. Isidore asked him to return to the world; however, Moses refused because he feared that he might return to his past, sinful ways. He asked St. Isidore to permit him to stay with them and to spend the rest of his life in the monastery. St. Isidore told him that the monastic life would be too difficult for him, but Moses replied, "I must try and struggle and prepare myself for heaven. As much as I have defiled and dirtied myself with sin, I must struggle to purify and clean my life in order to see God. I must now compensate for all the evils that I have previously done."

St. Isidore told him that life there would be too hard, and that the necessities are not readily available as in the world. Moses replied, "Help me with your prayers and guidance. Become a father to me, a guide, and a teacher." St. Isidore was joyous at Moses' steadfastness and took him to St. Macarius to prepare a new life for him.

St. Macarius then handed Moses back to St. Isidore to be ordained a monk and clothed with the monastic garb. He advised him, saying, "My son, stay in the wilderness and do not leave it, because the day you leave it, all the evils will return to you. Therefore, spend your entire life in it, and I believe that God will be merciful and gracious with you and will help you trample Satan under your feet."

Moses needed much encouragement and spiritual guidance, especially in the beginning. In this case, the spiritual guide is likened to a doctor, who can diagnose the illness and then prescribe the appropriate medicine. However, this also requires truthfulness, honesty, and obedience from the patient, and that is why the monastic fathers have always been meticulous in picking a spiritual guide, so that the person may not fall into the hands of a patient instead of a doctor.

The spiritual guide must have certain characteristics. He must have a pure and loving heart full of the Holy Spirit. He must also be patient, sincere, honest, a friend in times of trouble, and a partner in one's sorrows. Likewise, he must also be fair and not biased toward you or others. He cannot be bought with money or any allurement. He must be a good shepherd to his people and must be loyal to the Coptic Church. It is also said that the spiritual guide is not identified by old age and gray hair; rather, this gift and blessing are given by God to the person.

Moses continued to obey the true guidance of

St. Isidore and St. Macarius, who cared for every aspect of his life until his feet became steady on the rock of repentance. St. Isidore was his father of confession, and St. Macarius was his spiritual guide. The difference between the spiritual guide and the father of confession is that the spiritual guide is responsible for general spiritual guidance, while the father of confession takes confessions and gives absolutions for them. Oftentimes, the father of confession is also the spiritual guide.

How St. Moses Defeated Satan

Practice of Fasting and Prayer

As Moses continued in the life of fasting, prayer, and meditation, the devil that had been tempting him since his youth started to appear to him in terrifying ways. He fought him powerfully, especially through the desires of the flesh, until he almost lost hope and was going to return to his previous life. Moses informed St. Isidore of this warfare, to which St. Isidore responded, "Do not sorrow, because you are still in the beginning of the hardships. The tribulations will trouble your spirit for a long time, but do not lose heart. If you persevere in fasting and vigils, despise the raging lusts of the flesh, they will calm down, and the body will no longer request its old desires. The devil will depart from you in despair." Moses obeyed and continued in many practices that subdue the body, including eating very little bread once a day, and persisting in fasting and prayers as well as working much with his hands.

St. Moses said, "One day while I was fasting, I was tempted with the sin of adultery, so I entered deep into the desert and stayed there forty-two days. I rarely ate bread and drank water, and did not lie down or sit; I entreated God until He freed me from these temptations. After that, these lusts never tempted me again for the rest of my life."

His humility and not relying on his own righteousness or strength

St. Isidore told St. Moses, "Stop contending with the devils because there is a limit to courage even in ascetic struggle." He said this because, in the beginning, Moses lacked the knowledge of the principles of monastic life. Since he was physically strong, he struggled more than necessary, thinking that he could defeat the devils through his bravery, prayers, and fasting; he thought he could conquer and destroy the devils through his works alone. When the devils knew how he felt, they fought him continually with attacks, both secretly and openly; however, St. Isidore kept guiding him to obtain humility. He told him, "Without the power of the Holy Spirit through Communion and following the guidance of the father of confession and spiritual guide, victory is impossible."

Moses started to learn, and his thoughts became more and more humble. He took Communion and returned to his cell. He started fasting, praying, and working in moderation. Thus, he defeated the devils, and they reduced their battles against him. Since that time, he obtained rest and was filled with knowledge and peace.

Staying in His Cell and His Patience with its Sorrows

When adultery strongly tempted Moses, he was unable to stay in his cell, so he would go to St. Isidore and let him know. St. Isidore would give him advice and dismiss him. One night, he went to St. Isidore more than eleven times, and each time, St. Isidore would comfort him, pray for him, and send him back to his cell. Finally, St. Moses told him that he could not return to his cell, and at this, St. Isidore took him to the roof to show him an army of devils in the west and a multitude of God's angels in the east. He then said to Moses, "Look, they fight for us; those who are with us are greater than those against us." When Moses saw the scene before him, he was filled with joy, praised God, and returned to his cell encouraged.

His Wisdom in the Returning of Souls

At the beginning of his monastic life, four thieves from his old gang attacked St. Moses. The thieves found the cells to be easy targets because the cells were scattered across the mountain. The funny thing is that Moses captured them and tied all four of them together because he still had his bodily strength. He then presented them to the elders in the monastery to decide what to do with them. However, the elders told him to deal with the thieves himself. Moses was very gracious and kind to the thieves, and thus, they were touched. They were very surprised and full of joy when they discovered that their host was Moses, their former leader, the infamous thief. This led them to repentance at his hands. Some sources say that they followed him on the path of monasticism.

3

His Struggle in the Virtues

His Humility and Bearing Humiliations

A council was formed, and they wanted to test Moses the Strong, so they rebuked him, saying, "What is this black man doing among us?" When Moses heard this, he remained silent. At the end of the council, they questioned him, asking, "Why were you not upset?"

He replied, saying, "Truly, I was upset, but I did not speak."

Some of the brothers asked one of the elders about the meaning of what St. Moses said. The elder replied, "Monastic perfection is attained by two things: The first is calming the bodily senses, and the second is calming the senses of the soul. Calming the bodily senses occurs when the person accepts humiliation for the sake of Christ. He does not speak even though he is upset. As for silencing the senses of the soul, it occurs when he gets humiliated, but his soul does not become disturbed, and anger does not enter his heart."

Again, the Archbishop wanted to test him, so he asked the priests, "If Abba Moses comes to the church, cast him out, and let us see how he will respond." So when Moses entered the church, they yelled at him and cast him out, saying, "Get out of the church, you black-skinned man."

Moses went out saying to himself, "They have done well with you, O you black skinned man, since you are below humanity and are unworthy of sitting with people."

When the Archbishop heard his words, he ordained him a priest. After he was ordained, the people heard a voice saying, "Axios, Axios, Axios... Worthy, Worthy, Worthy."

It was also told that as he was ordained a priest and wore the white garment of service, one of the bishops said to him, "You have become white, O Moses." The saint replied, "I wish I were inwardly white as I am outwardly."

Fleeing from Vainglory

One day, the governor of the land heard about St. Moses' virtues, and he wished to see him. Therefore, he went to the wilderness of Scetis. St. Moses found out, and he was advanced in age. To escape from vainglory, he hid among the reeds of the swamp. As the governor and his honorable entourage were on the road, they met one of the elders in the wilderness. The governor said to him, "O you, old man, can you inform me of the location of St. Moses' cell?"

The elder replied, "What do you need to ask him? He is an old, incompetent man." This disturbed the governor, but he continued on his way until he arrived at the monastery where the elders were waiting for him.

He told them, "My fathers, I have heard a lot about St. Moses, and I have come to the desert to see him. On the way, I met an old man by the swamp, and I asked him about the location of St. Moses' cell. He replied, 'It is a hard path to the elder, and he is an incompetent man.'" These words that the governor spoke had a great impact on everyone, so they raised their voice and complained, saying, "Who is this insane old man who speaks in this manner about St. Moses, who is honored in all of Scetis?" The governor described him, saying, "He was a frail man, wearing long, beaten garments, who was blackened by the sun. He had a long white beard and was half bald." By his words, they understood the mystery, for the governor had met St. Moses himself, who had acted in this manner and described himself with these words. So the governor returned greatly edified.

His Asceticism

One day, when a group of people came from Egypt to see St. Moses, they saw a grilled snake prepared on St. Moses' table for lunch, and they were going to eat from it. However, St. Moses prevented them, saying, "This is an evil beast."

They asked him, "Why did you do this, O father?"

He replied, "My brothers, this poor soul desired fish, so I did this to extinguish its bad desire." The brothers were astonished, and they praised God who gave His saint this great grace.

Hiding His Canon and Keeping Christ's Commandment

It was once announced in Scetis to fast for a week. By coincidence, during that time, some visitors from Egypt came to visit St. Moses. He prepared a meal for them. When the nearby monks saw the smoke rising from his cell, they complained to the elder priests, saying that St. Moses had broken the command and prepared food. The elders assured them that they would speak to him on Saturday. When they spoke to him and found out the reason, they addressed him before the council and said, "Abba Moses, you have sacrificed the commandment of the people to keep God's commandment."

The Effectiveness of His Prayer

It is said that when he was starting to live in the cave that his spiritual father guided him to, he wondered, "How can I find water here for my needs?" He heard a voice saying, "Enter, and do not be worried." He dwelt there, and one day, some fathers came to visit him. He cooked lentil soup for them with the only jug of water he had. When he ran out of water, he became sad and paced in and out of the cave while praying to God. A rainy cloud came above the cave and started raining, and filled all his empty jugs. When he entered the cave, the fathers questioned him why he was pacing in and out. He answered them, "I was praying to God, saying, 'You are the one who has brought me to this place, and now I have no water for your servants to drink.' So I was pacing back and forth in prayer until God made it rain, and thus, we have received this water."

Serving Others and Escaping from Idleness

Transporting water to the cells was difficult at the time of St. Moses, because it was a long walk to the well. St. Moses took this chance and started to train himself in acts of love. He used to go out at night, collect the elders' jugs, and fill them with water. When the devil saw his good deeds, the devil left him alone for a while, until one day, as St. Moses came to the well, the devil beat him until his bones broke, and he lay down on the ground half-dead.

Some brothers came and carried him to the church, where he stayed for three days until he recovered.

Being Gentle and not Judging Sinners

It is said that one day, a brother from Scetis sinned, and a council was held to judge him. They sent for St. Moses to come to attend the council, but he refused to go, so the priest of the area went to him and told him, "All the fathers are waiting for you." St. Moses took a sack with a hole in it, filled it with sand, and carried it on his back as he went to the council. When the fathers saw him, they asked him, "What is this, father?" He answered them, "These are my sins, flowing freely behind my back, without me seeing them, and I have come today to judge another man for his sins." When the council heard this, they forgave the brother and did not upset him in any way.

His Martyrdom

One day, while the brothers were sitting around St. Moses, he told them, "The barbarians are coming to the wilderness, arise and escape."

They replied, "Will you not escape with us, father?"

He said, "I have been waiting for this day for many years so that the Savior's words might be fulfilled, 'for all who take the sword will perish by the sword.'"[8] This he said in reference to his previous sinful life.

Seven of the brothers told him, "We also will not escape and will die with you."

He replied, "As you wish. Each person must make their own decision, whether to run and live, or to remain and ascend to heaven."

After a short period of time, St. Moses said to them, "The barbarians are approaching the gate." The barbarians entered and killed them, but one brother was scared and hid among the reeds. Then he saw crowns descending from heaven onto the heads of the seven martyrs.

St. Moses left seventy of his disciples who followed his monastic path and teachings for many decades. He was martyred on the 24th of Paone and was more than eighty years old, twenty-five years of which were before he became a monk. The Coptic Church celebrates his departure on the 24th of Paone, which is the 1st of July. The Catholic, Greek, and Ethiopian churches commemorate his departure on the 28th of August.

---

8   Matthew 26:52.

4

Lessons Learned from the Life of St. Moses

The call of Heaven

God always sends us help, callings, and messages. These things can come to us from a sermon, a book, the story of a saint, or a friend. It may even come from a relative who tells us an inspiring story that reminds us of God's love for us and eternal life, and thus wakes us from the sea of sin in which we are drowning. We must be alert at all times and allow the Holy Spirit to work in us. We must take advantage of the opportunity to repent and return to God. Like St. Moses, when he heard the call of heaven, he seized the opportunity, repented without hesitation, and went to the wilderness of Scetis.

Not to be Shy in Confession

After the devil causes us to fall into the web of sin, he implants in us a shame of confessing our sin to our father of confession. He sends us thoughts of doubt, that we may think, "How can I say this sin to my father of confession, who respects me, sees me as a devout Christian, loves me, and whom I love dearly?" This will lead you to become ashamed of revealing your sins to your father of confession.

What is more preferable, revealing your sins to your father of confession, or revealing them to God and the multitudes on Judgment Day?

The father of confession is called a "father" because he can never become upset with you or think of you poorly, because you are his child in Christ and the Church, and he wishes to shape you into the perfect mold to hold the fullness of Christ.

To encourage yourself, remember that "there will be more joy in heaven over one sinner who repents than over ninety-nine just persons who need no repentance."[9]

After confession, look to the sky, and imagine the beautiful scene, the joy and praises of the choir of angels. The cherubim and the seraphim, along with all the saints, are rejoicing at your repentance. These can be a driving force for you to return to God, so do not sadden the angels, the cherubim,

---

9   Luke 15:7.

the seraphim, and all the saints by not returning. Imitate St. Moses the Strong when he confessed in the presence of all the monks because he only cared for the salvation of his soul and revealed all his sins.

Leaving Everything Related to Sin and the Old Life

It is known that every sin has various attachments, such as friends, places, and even some words, tools, or other elements that remind us of the sin. After completing repentance, we must distance ourselves from everything related to our past life, in order to avoid remembering anything concerning this sin. Hence, we pray in the Liturgy of St. Basil, "Cleanse us from…the remembrance of vice bearing death." Thus, we must entirely separate ourselves from all such things.

Seeking Your Father of Confession After Falling into Sin

After a person repents, the spiritual warfare becomes intensified by the forces of evil. If he falls into sin or even remembers the sin, he ought to hurry to his father of confession, because revealing the thoughts weakens the intensity of the attacks. That is what St. Moses did when thoughts of adultery attacked him more than eleven times in one night. St. Isidore comforted him each time and prayed for St. Moses, then sent him back to his cell.

Do not despair if you fall. Imitate the prodigal son and say, "I will arise and go to my father, and will say to him, Father, I have sinned against heaven and before you."[10]

Not to Depend on our Righteousness or our Works

Sometimes, after victory over our beloved sin, we rely on ourselves in the spiritual fight. We think that by our many fasts and prayers, we will prevail in our spiritual warfare. We forget that God is the One who gives us the victory over sin and leads us on the path of salvation through the Mysteries of the Church and the Holy Spirit. This is what St. Moses did when he relied on his physical might and large stature, and intensified his fasts and prayers without guidance.

A monastic elder once said, "Those without guidance fall like the leaves of a tree." This is what St. Isidore noticed when he saw St. Moses suffering from the frequency of spiritual battles. He said to him, "Stop contending with the devils because there is a limit to courage." He then gave him a suitable canon, which Moses obeyed and prevailed in all battles by the power of the Holy Spirit.

---

10   Luke 15:18.

5

The Sayings of St. Moses

✢ He who neglects the purity of his body will be ashamed in his prayer.

✢ Matters that stir anger in humans: arguing, fulfilling one's will, love of teaching, and thinking of oneself as wise.

✢ Elements that generate anger: dealings, negotiation, listening only to one's own voice, avoiding others' advice, and following one's desires.

✢ Do not be harsh on your brother, for we all get defeated by evil thoughts.

✢ Seek God, and you will find rest.

✢ He who remembers his sins and confesses them will not sin as often.

✢ He who thinks that he is flawless has contained in himself all the flaws.

✚ These are my sins trailing behind my back, unseen by me, and I have come today to judge another for his sins.

✚ No sin is without forgiveness, but that which is without repentance.

✚ It is better for a man to confess openly his thoughts; he who suppresses them will stir them against himself.

✚ Keeping the fear of God saves the soul from temptations.

✚ Prepare yourself to meet God, so that you may do His will.

✚ He who has the habit of talking in church has shown that God does not dwell in him.

✚ Seek repentance at all times and do not be idle for one moment.

✚ Pray at all times, and the Lord will shine in your heart.

✚ As termites rot the wood, so does sin to the soul.

✚ My beloved, as long as you have a chance, come back to Christ with a sincere repentance.

✚ A man who cannot guard his tongue is like a house without a door.

✚ Love the poor so that you may be saved in times of trial because of them.

✚ Four things keep the soul: showing mercy to

everyone, leaving anger, longsuffering, and casting out sins from the heart by praising God.

✢ Endure humiliation and sadness for the sake of Christ through humility and meekness of heart, placing before Him your weakness, and the Lord will become your strength.

✢ If lust becomes pleasant in your eyes, kill it with humility and take refuge in God, so you find rest. If you are tempted by the beauty of the body, remember its decay after death, and you will find rest.

✢ Humility of the heart precedes all virtues, and pride is the root of all evil.

✢ Let us hold fast to humility in every matter and every deed.

✢ Do not become proud and say, "Blessed am I," for you can never be confident about your enemies.

✢ Let us endure being cursed and insulted to get rid of pride.

✢ The soul's blindness comes from hatred of your brother, oppressing the poor, envy, and backbiting.

✢ Keep your hearing lest you gather sorrows to yourself.

✢ Keep your eyes pure lest hidden phantoms gather in your heart.

✤ Keep your tongue so that the fear of God may dwell in your heart.

✤ The fear of the Lord casts away all iniquities, and boredom casts away the fear of God.

✤ Let us use our tongues to remember God and justice, so that we may eliminate lying.

The Most Important Counsels and Sayings of St. Moses for Monks

✤ Examine yourself every day and meditate on which battles you have prevailed in. Do not trust in yourself, but say that mercy and support are from God.

✤ Do not think to yourself that you have excelled in righteousness until your last breath.

✤ If a man accepts to be blamed and admonished, then he shall gain humility.

✤ Forsaking one's work dims the mind, and tolerating and persevering in the toils enlighten the mind in God and strengthen the spirit.

✤ Six things defile the soul and the body: wandering in cities and villages, lack of control over the eyes, mingling with people of authority, acquainting women, love of materialistic talks, and vain words.

✤ Four are great help to the young monk: meditation every hour on God's commandments, keeping vigil, diligence in prayer, and considering oneself as nothing.

✤ Four are sources of darkening the mind: despising one's companion, hating him, envying him, and thinking the worse of him.

✤ Four things the mind needs every hour: continuous prayer with a worshipping heart, fighting the thoughts, considering oneself a sinner, and not judging anyone.

✤ Four lead to adultery: eating and drinking, oversleeping, idleness and being playful, and adornment with clothes.

✤ Four that are difficult to attain: Tears, thinking about one's sins, keeping death in front of one's eyes, and always saying, "I have sinned, forgive me."

✤ Three things are a support to the mind: To do good to those who wronged you, patience toward what your enemies do to you, and forsaking envy.

✤ Preservation from evil thoughts: reading in the books of commandments, abolishing laziness, waking up at night for prayers and praises, and always being humble.

✤ Three that help us reach heaven: Grief and sorrow, weeping over sins and trespasses, and expecting death every day and every hour.

✤ The most important weapon of virtue is

wearying the body with discernment. Laziness and slothfulness bring warfare.

✤ Weary your body lest you be ashamed in the resurrection of the righteous.

✤ If you dwell with the brethren, do not order them to do what needs to be done, but toil with them so that your reward will not be lost.

✤ Do not love comfort as long as you are in this life.

✤ Beware of idleness so as not to be sorry, but rather work with your hands so that you provide for the poor, because idleness is death and a fall for the soul.

✤ If anyone keeps these, whether dwelling in a monastery or as a solitary or in the world, he can be saved:

1. As it is written: one should love God with all their spirit and all their mind.

2. One should love their neighbor as oneself.

3. One should die to all evil.

4. One should not judge his brother in any matter.

5. One should do no evil to anyone.

6. Before departing from the body, one should purify oneself from all the defilements of the body and the spirit.

7. One should always have a broken and humble heart. He can achieve this through constant focus on his sins and not others' sins with the help of Jesus Christ, who lives and reigns with the Father and the Holy Spirit unto the end of the ages. Amen.

✤ One cannot be a soldier in the army of Christ unless he becomes all fire, despising glory and comfort, breaking ties of lust, and keeping all the commandments of God.

✤ He also said: "It is impossible to attain Jesus except by struggle, humility, and unceasing prayer."

✤ He used to also say: "If one neglects his inner work, his mind is darkened, but he who perseveres in his work, his thoughts are in God and his spirit is strengthened and fortified."

✤ He also said: "The monk who is close to God and has a relationship with Him succeeds in letting no one into his cell."

✤ And on obedience to the spiritual guide, he said: "Let us acquire obedience that gives birth to humility and brings perseverance, patience, self-reproach, brotherly love, and compassion. Truly, these are our weapons in our spiritual warfare."

✤ He also said: "Brother, let us walk in true obedience as it is the cause of humility, strength, joy, perseverance, patience, brotherly love, self-reproach, and compassion, as this is the righteous obedience that fulfills all of God's commandments."

✤ He also said: "A monk who is under the guidance of an elder father and does not practice obedience and humility, will not attain a single virtue and will not even know what a monk is."

Appendix: Hymns for Abba Moses the Strong

A Hymn for Abba the Strong

✤ He who remembers his sins: And turns to God: The heaven rejoices for him: *The strong Abba Moses.*

✤ A sinner who strayed: His steps were all evil: He drank sin like water: *The strong Abba Moses.*

✤ Satan blinded him with lust: He seduced him like the serpent: His eyes were blinded: *The strong Abba Moses.*

✤ He asked, "Where is God?: Is He in this rock?: On earth or in heaven": *The strong Abba Moses.*

✤ The Lord called him: He led him to Shiheet: And revived his life: *The strong Abba Moses.*

✤ He saw Abba Isidore: He spoke to him about Jesus: Christ, the Holy One: *The strong Abba Moses.*

✣ He believed upon his words: He wept for his past: And repented for it: *The strong Abba Moses.*

✣ He met Abba Macarius: He confessed with all regret: So the Lord showed a sign: *The strong Abba Moses.*

✣ Behold, an angel came: With him, a black tablet: He erased it and made it white: *The strong Abba Moses.*

✣ The Lord heard your voice: He accepted your tears: He erased all your sins: *The strong Abba Moses.*

✣ The past, our Lord Jesus covered: He forgave it with His Blood: He forgot it as He said: *The strong Abba Moses.*

✣ The lion became a lamb: He became a role model: The Lord's work is fulfilled: *The strong Abba Moses.*

✣ O faithful struggler: Against the demonic wars: As the years pass by: *The strong Abba Moses.*

✣ They fought you with thoughts: With pride and self-image: And desires, day and night: *The strong Abba Moses.*

✣ He refused to be a judge: Over a monk who sinned: He said, "I am like him": *The strong Abba Moses.*

✣ The teacher by example: Before the monks, he raised: A broken bag with sand: *The strong Abba*

Moses.

✜ He said, "These are my sins: The ignorance of my youth: How can I judge my brother": *The strong Abba Moses.*

✜ O treasure of virtues: He conquered vainglory: And felt very lowly: *The strong Abba Moses.*

✜ A monk in the fear of God: Does not condemn his brother: His eyes towards heaven: *The strong Abba Moses.*

✜ As the father of fathers: He welcomes the strangers: He is a generous giver: *The strong Abba Moses.*

✜ As Elijah in prayer: When he needed water: The heaven rained water: *The strong Abba Moses.*

✜ Your words are a great treasure: To all the Christians: Hermits and worshipers: *The strong Abba Moses.*

✜ On July first, a feast: Of a chosen martyr: In the assembly of the righteous: *The strong Abba Moses.*

✜ O martyr of Jesus Christ: To you, praise is sweet: With one voice we proclaim: "*The strong Abba Moses.*"

✜ O Abba Moses, the hero: You are our role model: In our life with zeal, *The strong Abba Moses.*

✜ Visitors come to the abbey: In their hearts, giving thanks: Proclaiming to you, saying: "*The strong Abba Moses."*

✤ O blessing for the clergy: O beloved of the Lord Jesus: Living in Paradise: *The strong Abba Moses.*

✤ In Texas and Baramous: Brothers, monks and priests: Saying, "Axios": *The strong Abba Moses.*

✤ Remember our Pope: Abba Tawadros the beloved: And Abba Youssef, our Metropolitan: *The strong Abba Moses.*

✤ Likewise, I the sinner: Pray for my salvation: Of my weakness and lusts: *The strong Abba Moses.*

Another Hymn for Abba Moses the Strong

1. In the Church of the firstborn: In the pure assembly: Living in all piety: *The strong Abba Moses.*

2. He was an idol worshipper: A highway robber: He inquired about the Judge: *The strong Abba Moses.*

3. Moses was a barbarian: His life was full of sin: He yearned to be purified: *The strong Abba Moses.*

4. A thief, murderer, and adulterer: Lover of this passing world: The precious Blood washed him: *The strong Abba Moses.*

5. Moses the thirsty heard: Of our fathers the monks: The dwellers of Shiheet: *The strong Abba Moses.*

6. He asked, "Is there a God: Great and awesome?: My heart yearns for Him": *The strong Abba Moses.*

7. Abba Isidore answered: "Our God is strong and Holy: All heads bow to Him": *The strong Abba Moses.*

8. "Our God is merciful: He took the form of man: Through love, He accepted shame": *The strong Abba Moses.*

9. "Our God's promises are true: He accepts the repentant: And He loves the broken hearted": *The strong Abba Moses.*

10. "Give your life to Him: Abandon your past with Him: with His grace repent to Him": *The strong Abba Moses.*

11. Moses stood and said: "Receive me like a lost son: Help me to repent now!": *The strong Abba Moses.*

12. With tears and joy: With groaning and delight: He repented of his past: *The strong Abba Moses.*

13. He approached Christ with love: Heartbroken and wounded: He wished to gain rest: *The strong Abba Moses.*

14. He offered a true repentance: Openly without turning back: Revealing all his sins: *The strong Abba Moses.*

15. Lo, an angel of light: Wiped away his black sins:

The tablet became pure white: *The strong Abba Moses.*

16. Abba Macarius witnessed: That his Lord forgave and saved him: A new life was granted him: *The strong Abba Moses.*

17. He received the first Mystery: By water, Spirit and fire: Removing all impurities: *The strong Abba Moses.*

18. Repentance is amazing: Kindling fire in the heart: The stranger becomes a companion: *The strong Abba Moses.*

19. The murderer became righteous: The sinner, a chosen vessel: The robber, among the chosen ones: *The strong Abba Moses.*

20. Repentance is powerful: Making the adulterous a virgin: And the rebellious, accepted: *The strong Abba Moses.*

21. A servant of desires and shame: Received dignity though grace: Becoming the strongest of the free: *The strong Abba Moses.*

22. The Spirit guided the tyrant: From darkness to light: Producing fruits for His beloved: *The strong Abba Moses.*

23. He longed for monasticism: And vowed to walk in goodness: God showed him the way: *The strong Abba Moses.*

24. His asceticism surpassed others: He served the

other monks: With humility and vigils: *The strong Abba Moses.*

25. With perseverance, he exhausted himself: Walking thousands of meters: To fill their water jars: *The strong Abba Moses.*

26. He was advancing in the way: In steadfastness and diligence: And growth in righteousness: *The strong Abba Moses.*

27. In virtues and prayers: In fasting and asceticism: In reverence and prostrations: *The strong Abba Moses.*

28. An ascetic faithful worshiper: With strong steadfast faith: Terrifying the demons: *The strong Abba Moses.*

29. He loved the brothers and was loved: They chose him for the priesthood: They made known their desire: *The strong Abba Moses.*

30. When they tested him: The priests roused and expelled him: He submitted to their command: *The strong Abba Moses.*

31. He said, "I am not worthy: They banished you, O black one: O you, dark-skinned man!": *The strong Abba Moses.*

32. The patriarch heard his sayings: He learned of his righteous acts: His humble and perfect soul: *The strong Abba Moses.*

33. He ordained him in the holy Name: A voice said

"Axios!": All the souls heard it: *The strong Abba Moses.*

34. Blessed are you, O Moses!: You received your King's praise: The Lord of the vine protected you: *The strong Abba Moses.*

35. Once they requested you: For the case of a sinful monk: In the assembly they would judge him: *The strong Abba Moses.*

36. Saint Moses came to them: A bag of sand on his back: He entered sad and depressed: *The strong Abba Moses.*

37. They asked him what he carried: What is it that he brought in: He said he is carrying his sins: *The strong Abba Moses.*

38. A famous helpful lesson: The monks accepted joyfully: They forgave the poor sinner: *The strong Abba Moses.*

39. We wish to live your life: We wish to be like you: Remember us in your prayers: *The strong Abba Moses.*

40. Before the exalted throne: Before God the great: Remember us, our beloved father: *The strong Abba Moses.*

41. Pope Abba (...) the great: May God grant him long life: To preach the Gospel: *The strong Abba Moses.*

42. Abba (...) our bishop: Keep him and us, O

Lord: With his prayers, protect us: *The strong Abba Moses.*

43. The bishops and clergy: Guard them, O Holy One: With the ranks of the Angels: *The strong Abba Moses.*

44. The deacons and monks: The servants in every place: Lord, fill them with faith: *The strong Abba Moses.*

45. Abba Moses, blessed are you: You received your King's praise: The Lord of the vine protected you: *The strong Abba Moses.*

46. The mention of your name: Is in all the believers' mouths: They all say "O God of Abba Moses: Help all of us!"

Bibliography

An Article on Abba Moses by the late Abba Ghregorius, Bishop for Scientific Research.

Bishop Macari as of Minya, *Al-Qawi Al-Qidees Al-Anba Moussa Al-As'wad* [The Strong Saint, Abba Moses the Elack]. (Egypt: 2006).

Bustan Al-Rohban [Paradise of the Monks]. (Egypt: Diocese of Beni Swef and Bahnasa, 1976).

Bustan Al-Rohban Al-Mowasah, Al-joz' Al-Awal [The Expanded Paradise of the Monks, Vol. 1]. (Egypt: St. Macarius Monastery, 2006).

John of Sinai, *At-Sullam Ila Alalh* [The Ladder of Divine Ascent]. (Egypt: The Library of the Monastery of the Syrians, 1996).

The Coptic Synaxarion

www.ingramcontent.com/pod-product-compliance
Lightning Source LLC
Chambersburg PA
CBHW021226020426
42331CB00003B/494